Brennen I heard
You enjoy looking for
things in the woods So
I thought this book is
Just for You.
Enjoy!
 - Brad BeLK

A WALK
THROUGH THE WOODS
OF MINNESOTA

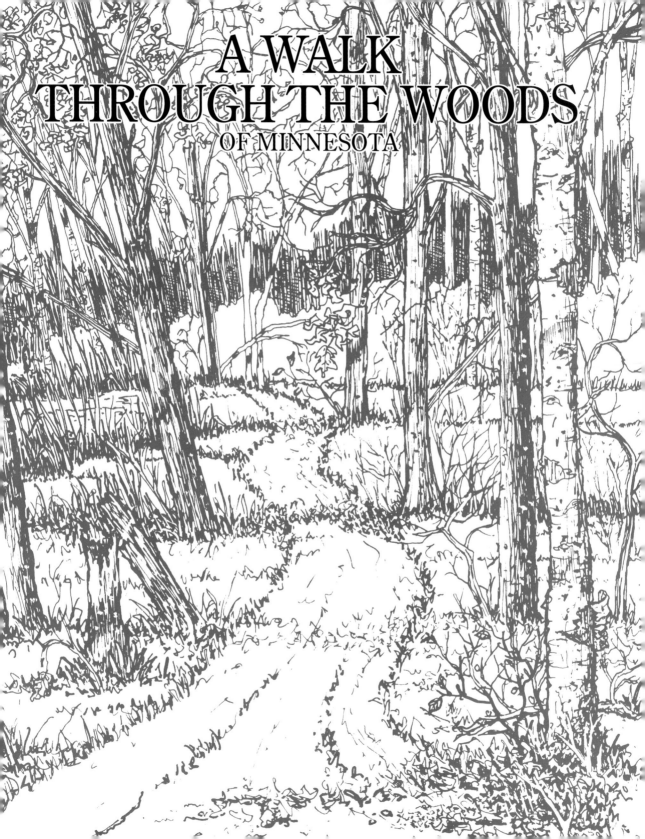

A Walk Through The Woods Of Minnesota. Original Idea by Gene and Jeanne Melich Gangelhoff.
Illustrations by Gene Gangelhoff. Written by Jeanne Melich Gangelhoff and Bradford Belk.

Please write with any comments or requests.
G J & B Publishing
P.O. Box 3301
Mpls., MN 55403

Library of Congress Registration No. TXU 502 456
ISBN: 0-9635006-0-0
Second printing: May 1993
Printed in the United States of America
Printed By Gopher State Litho, Minneapolis, Minnesota
Printed on Acid Free Paper

A Walk Through The Woods Of Minnesota

A walk through the woods will bring
an unexpected awareness:
the smells, sounds and sights will bathe your spirit,
and these precious recollections
will enhance your memory.
The deer striking a delicate pose by birch trees,
a fox snooping through underbrush
and rabbits peeking out of snug hutches.
The wood, mallard and teal ducks with noble heads
iridescent and high, add their touch of continuity
tucking their families under wing.
All of these create a majestic painting,
a gift to remember.

Cottontail Rabbit

I entered the woods
and immediately noticed some
movement beneath a beautiful birch
tree up ahead to my left. I stopped and
observed a cottontail rabbit with its
protective brownish-gray coat,
sniffing about. I was confident
more cottontails were in the
area. Favorite homes
include thickets and
briar patches.

$\mathcal{M}$allard Duck

As I continued on
my path, a pond came
into view. I hastened my pace
to get there. I spied a pair of gorgeous
mallard ducks. Common throughout
Minnesota, the mallard duck commands a
beauty and majesty which few in the wild
can claim. The male has an unmistakable
green or bluish-black head with a white
band encompassing the neck. Usually
found near water, but preferring
refuge in weeds, bulrushes
and cattails.

$\mathscr{C}$anada Goose

Further down the trail I
saw two Canada geese, gliding
silently through the water as though
not even there. It is a sure sign of spring
or autumn when thousands can be seen
migrating. They are found in water from the
largest lake in Minnesota to the
smallest stream. A true
wildlife beauty.

Ringneck Pheasant

The path turned to the
right and I followed. An open
field came into view with several
beautiful pheasants appearing. The
pheasant is one of the most popular
game birds in the upper midwest. Both
sexes have short rounded wings and
a long pointed tail. The cocks, with
color as abundant as a rainbow,
find territories in the spring
and are joined by several
hens in the fall.

$\mathscr{B}$eaver

As the path rounded the end
of the pond, I heard a faint slap resonate
along the birch-lined shore. I stopped in my
tracks, motionless, as my eyes scanned back
at the water. I spotted a beaver, parting the
water as he swiftly maneuvered his way with
his paddle-shaped tail. Suddenly he dove
underwater en route to the shared colonies
called domes, where the beavers' offspring are
raised. Remnants of fallen birch and poplar
trees lay on the shoreline, serving as a
reminder of the months of hard work
the beaver endures in building
their domes.

Chipmunk

Racing past the trail and
stopping on a fallen log, the
striped chipmunk poses for a
moment. Alarmed by anyone's
presence, he scurries along, always
in search of acorns for his hibernation
in the winter months. The chipmunk
sleeps and stores food in his shallow
burrow. Although legend says
he is safe from other animals,
the chipmunk does
have predators.

*R*ed Fox

As I continued, I thought I
saw something to my left. I stopped
and studied, spotting a red fox dashing
on a fence behind two oaks. Often
hunted, this sleek animal knows how to stay
alive by ducking into any small opening.
Mating occurs in January and February
with a litter of four to ten pups arriving
in about 50 days. The next time
you see a quick blur in the
woods, it could very
well be the red fox.

Whitetail Deer

Near the end of my walk through
the woods I saw a whitetail deer standing
alone on an animal trail. When running, the
whitetail deer is as smooth as an artist's brush
stroke on canvas. Full-grown adults can weigh up
to 400 pounds and measure six feet from nose
to tail. Favorite residences include creek
bottoms, cornfields, woods and forest
boundaries. A pleasurable final
sighting on my walk through
the woods of Minnesota.

Tracking Tips

1. Be very quiet when walking to see animals.

2. Wear dull or camouflage clothing so you are not as noticeable.

3. Stop and stand very still for a couple of minutes or longer, this way you can hear the different sounds of the woods and animals. Sometimes birds will come closer to investigate you. They are curious too.

4. Take a close look at the ground to see the different tracks. Watch for signs like gnawed trees, tufts of fur, chewed branches and buds. Watch for different animal markings.

5. For fun, match the following eight animals to their tracks. Answers are on the bottom of the next page.

A. _____   B. _____

C. _____

D. _____

E. _____

F. _____

G. _____

H. _____

A. Beaver B. Chipmunk C. Whitetail Deer D. Cottontail Rabbit E. Mallard Duck F. Red Fox
G. Pheasant H. Canada Goose

Our Trip To The Woods

There are many more animals in the woods and at any
given time you may meet several of them.
For your convenience, we've included a list of animals you
will want to be on the lookout for.
It's fun to discover our wildlife
and to protect it. Be sure and set aside some time
and take your walk through the woods today.

Day_____   Month_____   Year_____

_____Bear   _____Moose

_____Beaver   _____Pheasant

_____Canada Goose   _____Red Fox

_____Chipmunk   _____Red Tail Hawk

_____Cottontail Rabbit   _____Skunk

_____Elk   _____Timberwolf

_____Loon   _____Whitetail Deer

_____Mallard Duck   _____Woodchuck

_____   _____

_____   _____

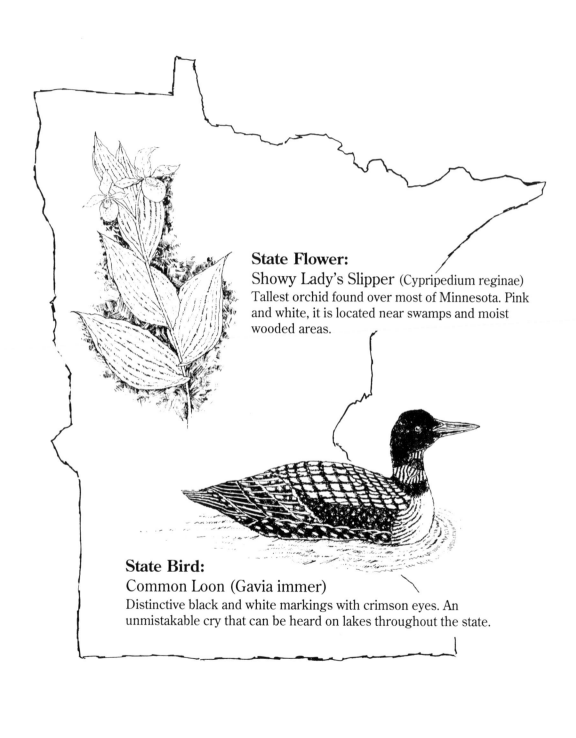

State Flower:
Showy Lady's Slipper (Cypripedium reginae)
Tallest orchid found over most of Minnesota. Pink
and white, it is located near swamps and moist
wooded areas.

State Bird:
Common Loon (Gavia immer)
Distinctive black and white markings with crimson eyes. An
unmistakable cry that can be heard on lakes throughout the state.

Inspirations

About The Authors

Gene and Jeanne Gangelhoff have been artists throughout their lives and enjoy nature and wildlife in their native land of Minnesota. Jeanne has also enjoyed writing short stories through the years. Talented in oil and watercolor, they like to depict the natural habitat Minnesota is noted for. Also fond of their domestic animals, they feel the necessity to protect all species.

Bradford Belk has resided in North Dakota, South Dakota, Utah and Minnesota. With a deep appreciation for the outdoors he enjoys journeys into the country and woods. Brad thanks his immediate and extended families for their immense support. As Proverbs 4:26 says, "Take heed to the path of your feet, then all your ways will be sure".

The authors wish to acknowledge their deep appreciation
to the following for their support of
A Walk Through The Woods Of Minnesota.
Their contributions to the project helped
our dream become reality.

Marian Melich
Lyle and Virginia Belk
Jim and Cris Haines
In memory of Leonard Melich

Gene and Linda Taylor
Eddie and Jean Fuerstenberg
Brian Jon Fuerstenberg
Bob and Shirl Smith
Milt and Phyllis Daline
Dick and Beverly LeVoir
Alexander Scott Nord
Paul and Binie Bertils
Melvin and Genevieve Bodine
Mary Tarver
John and Joni Belk
Bob and Susan Hylland
Peter Haines
Jennifer Murphy
Kenny and Alex Horst
In memory of Vernon and Eva Belk
In memory of Jewell Tarver